When Tulips Bloom:
A Personal Guide for Blossoming Through The Difficult
Seasons of Life

Stephanie R. Strong

...your present circumstance,
even through the most extreme conditions of life's transitions, is
just a temporary period that God uses to
grow you from a fall season of dormancy to a spring season full of
beautiful incredible blossoms.

DEDICATION:

This book is dedicated to my one and only daughter, Charisse Ange'le Rox Felton, who has been a source of encouragement in more ways than I can number. Your constant prayers, listening ear, willingness to provide objective critique, and feedback have been priceless. Your youthful wisdom is to be envied. Without you Charisse, the many lessons of this book would have gone unlearned and unshared. You are a beautiful young woman of God, an awesome wife, an amazing mother, and a diamond of a daughter. You are my greatest gift of joy! I thank God for every thought of you.

With love, Mommy

Acknowledgements

Hands down, this book would have never come to birth had it not been for the One Person who gave it to me. I must thank God for giving me the title one early spring morning over two and a half years ago. I thank God for the myriad of experiences and life lessons through which He has strengthened me, held me together, and confirmed His love over and over again. It has been through the agency of His Spirit that inspired and guided me to pen the thoughts that He wanted to share with you in this book. I thank God! I could end right here and it would be sufficient. However, I'd like to acknowledge some groups of people who have been instrumental in pouring into me over the past four years. If I list names, I know I will forget someone. You will know who you are when you read these acknowledgements. I want to honor my parents who have done their best in teaching me values and the meaning of perseverance. I'd like to thank some very *special* family members who have believed in me, listened to me cry, with whom I've shared my inner most thoughts, and to those who have offered encouraging words of support during this process. To my grandmother, you are my entire heartbeat! I am so thankful to have you in my life! To my godparents/god-family, you have blessed me with your love and support my entire life, I am so grateful! I have girlfriends who have listened to me pour my heart out about the journey on which I have been tasked to travel. You have been supportive on many levels. I heart you! To all my clients, your support has been nothing short of phenomenal! Thank you for hanging in there with me. To the hundreds and hundreds of people who have read, liked, commented, and shared my posts on social media over the years, you have been a blessing to me in more ways than you know. My church family, what can I say? Thank you for helping me to grow spiritually and for giving me a platform to hone my God-given gifts. To all of my newly acquired friends, you have given me new life on all the adventures we have shared together. During my time of extreme difficulty, God placed some very special people who became ministering angels to aid me when times were tough. You stepped right in and demonstrated what love does. I thank you from the depth of my heart. I'd like to thank my eleventh hour crew. You know who you are. Thank you for stopping by my job, reading, reviewing, editing, critiquing, and encouraging me up to the minute. I am so blessed by your generosity. Finally, I thank you all for being my teachers. Life with you has been my ever-learning classroom! May God be ever so gracious to you!

Much Love, Steph

Contents

INTRODUCTION:

As I was out for a morning run, my eyes caught something beautiful, something wonderful, something refreshing, something that appeared in full blossom almost out of nowhere. It was a bed of amazing tulips. I'm sure everyone has seen tulips at least once in their lifetime. Tulips are bulbous flowers that are planted in the early fall season of the year in order to bloom at the beginning of spring. Because of its natural homeland weather conditions of extremely hot arid summer temperatures, and bitterly cold winters, tulips possess a specialized method of remaining dormant during the dark freezing cold; and solely rely on its ability to draw from its underground storage bulbs to survive the most extreme conditions.

Like tulip bulbs, we humans sometimes go through extreme conditions. Extreme conditions occur when the unimaginable happens; when there is a drastic change in life's circumstances; when the fear of dread, the unknown, doubt, or maybe even regret paralyzes a person's faith in hopes that a better day is coming, and that a change is even possible.

If you have found yourself somewhere between "I don't believe this is happening to me" and "When will this be over for me?", then this book offers good news for you. There is no circumstance, season, storm, or condition that lasts always. Change can happen, but not without transition. Have you been feeling like you are in the middle of a serious transition in your life? Have you been crying out that something has got to give? Hoping that something new or greater is in your future or on the horizon? Have you been feeling a sense of urgency? Are you feeling that things are moving too slow or not at all? These are common questions and thoughts that people have when transitioning from one phase of life to the next. I would like to call these transitions, seasons. We humans can experience a range of seasons in a short period of time or over an extended period of time ranging from a season of thriving to a season of barely making it from day to day. In this book, the life cycle of the beautiful tulip is used as a metaphor to give you a visual of the process of surviving life's transitions. Much like tulip bulbs, many people may experience being in the fall and winter seasons of their life, when everything seems dormant and cold; chilling and unmoving; when there seems to be no activity of the Creator moving on their behalf; when what was once green, growing, alive and thriving in their life, now seems to be lifeless, dreary, gray, and hopeless. Since tulips have the capacity to rely on its underground storage for survival, it is not unimaginable to think that you do too. During your darkest, coldest, apparently stagnant moments, you will have to solely rely on the underground storage of God's supply. It is during these times that God uses challenging circumstances and extreme conditions to serve as soil for latent bulbs that He plants in our seasons of distress and disappointment.

If you are in that season, then you're going to love this book. Even though you may not realize or see what is going on deeply beneath the surface of your life's difficulties, root system activity is still being established. Don't become discouraged just because you don't see anything happening on the surface, because beneath the surface, God is engaged in doing root system work. God continues to nourish the roots of your life so that you are able to solely rely on Him. While He is working on your roots, He gives you just enough nourishment for you to draw strength and increase your faith so that you can become more dependent on Him. He still gives you creativity, leads you to resolve, paints your life with brilliance, and helps you foster new patterns of behavior from the underground storage that He had already established within you. On the surface, you may look at yourself and think that you are barely surviving, but barely surviving to God only gives Him cause to set the precedence for you to thrive. He is your Gardener and your Guide.

This book is a personal guide to help you through many of life's difficulties, and to help you better understand that your present circumstance, even through the most extreme conditions of life's transitions, is just a temporary period that God uses to guide you from a dormant fall season of bareness to a spring season of beautiful incredible blossoms. Come along and grow with me on this incredible journey called: When Tulips Bloom!

Chapter 1
What Brings You HERE!

You have arrived at a very interesting place: HERE!

How many times have you rehearsed in your mind how

different things are now? The soul-searching, the pause at

a major cross-road in your life, the feeling of discontent

seem to be on repeat. Maybe you are feeling apathetic

about things for which you once had passion, which

ultimately have left you with a whole lot of unanswered

questions, some disappointments, or perhaps confusion? If

it is any consolation to you at all, you are not alone. Like

many of us, you arrived at this place, this spot, this time

for a reason. Often times, when life tends to get a little

fuzzy, and a person begins to ask questions, such as, "Who

am I?" - "What am I here for?" - "Why aren't I happy?" –

"When will this all end?" – "When will I get my turn?" –

"How could I have done that?" – "What am I really

supposed to be doing?" – "What am I supposed to do next?

usually signify that a change is getting ready to take place.

Change is typically on the horizon when tension builds up.

The tension manifests itself when an individual becomes

uncomfortable about where they are mentally, spiritually,

physically, relationally, or vocationally. This state of being

uncomfortable stirs up successive introspective inquiring

about the meaning of life. Some people inquire about how

they are wired, what makes them genuinely happy, what

adds the most meaning and value to their life, or how they

are measuring or evaluating their own success. If neither

of these questions has come across your mind, then I am

pretty certain that you have at least been thinking about

something that has brought you to a place of inquiry! And

quite frankly, in my opinion, that is a very good place to start.

I am not going to speculate by attempting to know exactly where you are. But if you are asking questions, then I can relate because I was once at a place of inquiry. This is where self-discovery begins. This is where I started. Now I cannot pinpoint the exact time, place, or circumstance that emoted this seemingly uncomfortable state, but I believe what matters most importantly is that the place to which I came was prompted by a series of questions I began asking myself, while trying to find answers simultaneously. Since I didn't have all the answers, I just pushed all the thoughts, denials, and contradictions to the back of my mind until another impulse brought me back to that familiar place of inquiry again and again. If you are wrestling in the same experience, I am suggesting that the promptings, urges, impulses, or whatever it is that continues to nudge at you, may be God's way of getting your attention so that you can be proactive in your solution. Renee Swope observes, "Sometimes God answers our prayers by calling us to be part of the solution to our problems. Instead of changing our circumstances, often God uses our circumstances to change us by bringing us closer to Him, making us more like Him, and helping us find our confidence in Him." (Swope, 2013) With that being said, our circumstances are communication channels in which I believe God calls us into relationship, conversation, and intimacy with Him.

As God has initiated communication with you by way of your circumstances, what questions have you been asking lately? To whom have you been asking? What challenges are you facing? What mindset have you adapted? I ask these questions because I want you to really think about who you are. I want you to think about whether you feel accepted, appreciated, successful, or valued. Give yourself permission to ask questions and seek answers.

If you are like me, you have had your share of life's difficulties. Listen, I have gotten tired of making the same decisions and choices over and over again without experiencing success? Have you been feeling like that as well? I know I have. Whatever you may be feeling or thinking about your current situation, the fulfillment of your life is best realized when you understand why you are here. It is important to know the value of your life.

When you don't know your value, you will accept almost anything to define it. When you accept anything or any truth that is an imposter of your true value, it will cause you to raise questions of doubt, self-worth, purpose, love, and acceptance. These questions are imbedded in your fears: fear of failing, fear of being exposed, fear of abandonment, fear of letting your guard down, fear of being misunderstood, fear of lack, etc.

Sometimes, we have to ask ourselves these hard questions, so that we can become a part of the solution. What is very critical in this stage is for you to be patient with yourself. If your focus is only on the end result, you may miss a very important development process. Becoming a part of your own solution involves being *proactive in that process*. Being proactive also means asking critical questions that make you dig deep for the answers. No one is going to give you the answers that you need. The answers are already within you. So be brave enough to ask yourself necessary questions! To assist you with this process, I have formulated some questions that will help guide you in discovering your answers.

    A. On the lines below, describe a memorable time in your life when you consider yourself to be happy and content?

_____

_____

_____

_____

_____

_____

_____

_____

_____

_____

_____

_____

_____

B. On the lines below, describe a time in your life
   when you considered yourself to be the most
   disappointed?

_____

_____

_____

_____

_____

_____

_____

_____

_____

_____

_____

C. On the lines below, write down your personal values, i.e., honesty, reliable, etc…?

_____

_____

_____

_____

D. How do you motivate yourself? Describe the best way others can motivate you in relationship, at work, or working with a group? Then describe the best way you or anyone else can deflate your motivation?

_____

_____

_____

_____

_____

E. What keeps you moving forward when you want to quit?

_____

_____

_____

_____

F. What makes you quit when you really want to move forward?

_____

_____

_____

_____

These questions are designed to help you identify areas where you may have had limiting beliefs about yourself or your capabilities. Some people acknowledge this state as being "stuck'. By recognizing the areas of limitation, you become better equipped to neutralize them with positive affirming beliefs. I dare to say that just about everyone deals with at least one hidden thing within that they believe keeps or has kept them from being the successful, healthy, happy person they know they can be or desire to be. It doesn't matter your race, religion, economic status, affluence, or affiliations…. you will find that that there are many successful people who appear to excel without limitations. Then, you will find those who allow every limitation to keep them from excelling. Well of course, there are those in the middle who have had some success, but still may not be content, healthy, or happy in either area. As you read earlier, you are not alone. Remember: we were created to thrive-- not merely survive. By the end of this chapter, it is my desire that you would have moved closer to identifying hidden hindrances that impede your progress, and ultimately get you thinking in the direction that you would like to go in order to maximize your God-given potential.

Your God-given potential is to be capitalized, not minimized. There are several ways to look at what's holding you back. Let's start with the idea that "technically" no one or nothing is holding you back. No one or nothing has you in restraints. The unfortunate thing about delayed dreams is that somehow people end up talking themselves out of the very thing they want to do. I blog frequently at presencewithpurpose.net. One of the most recurring questions I ask is "What are you telling yourself?" We are more apt to believe what we are telling ourselves more than what others tell us. If you are, by chance, handing yourself a great big serving of negativity, then there's no wonder why you have allowed yourself to be *detained* by that same heaping of negativity. If you are telling yourself, "They won't give me a promotion or a chance," then there's no wonder you probably have stopped believing in yourself, and started believing that "they" have the power to keep you back. If you have been telling yourself that "I do not have time," or "It's too difficult," or "I don't see how I am going to be able to do this," then where you are now is the direct result of what you have confirmed to yourself. Stop confirming negativity. You hold yourself back when you do this. So, the first thing in this exercise that I'd like for you to do is...

1. Develop new thoughts that allow you to converse with yourself affirmatively. Here's how: Think

of a traffic light. When the light has turned yellow, that is your cue to slow down and prepare to stop. Right? Well, when a thought enters your mind that could create a negative conversation with yourself about what you want to do with your life, consider it a "yellow light." Slow down your thoughts, and prepare to stop them in its tracks. Every time you rehearse progress-impeding thoughts, you invariably begin to meditate on them. What we meditate on soon becomes our reality. That's why the Scriptures give instruction on how to have a healthy and positive mind. Philippians 4:8 states, "Finally, brethren, whatsoever things are true, whatsoever things are honest, whatsoever things are just, whatsoever things are pure, whatsoever things are lovely, whatsoever things are of good report; if there be any virtue, and if there be any praise, think on these things." It doesn't get any clearer than this. Regardless of your belief system, if you want to stop negative self-talk, then you will have to replace those bad thoughts with thoughts that promote healing, happiness, and wholeness. Many of today's most prolific counselors, coaches, clergy, and thought leaders teach that what you give the most focused attention to, you consequently create that reality. So the most important thing to remember about changing your thought process and internal conversation with yourself and others is to replace negative thoughts with thoughts that are reflected in Philippians 4:8 above. Now, this strategy takes practice. However, you owe it to yourself to develop it. Nothing more, nothing less. *In section I on the lines below, write down your typical thoughts or responses when things are not going well. In section II, write an affirming thought or affirmation that will counter or neutralize your original response.*

For example:

I. Typical response: When it seems like I can't ever get it right, I often tell myself that "I am a failure". (negative self talk)

II. Affirming response: When it seems like I can't ever get it right, I will tell myself, "I am successfully working toward a solution and open to trying another approach."(healthy self-talk)

Your turn:

I.   Typical response:_____

_____

_____

II. Affirming Response:_____

_____

_____

2. The second strategy I would like for you to try is to "set your intention." You do this probably more than you realize. Setting your intention is equivalent to setting your *internal GPS*. This means you have to determine what it is (in specific terms) you want to accomplish or where you want to go. Your intention is fuel and power. It carries a positive charge, whether it is for good or for bad. Every action begins with an intention. If you are tired of acting or reacting in the same counter-productive ways, then it starts with setting your intention. Once you have cleared that up, then you can begin to unpack your ideas, establish a plan, and take steps towards any goal or aspiration. I can assure you that once you make up your mind and set your intention, you will be guided in the direction of the energy you expend to make this accomplishment possible. When we get serious about the direction we want our lives to go, God will get serious about helping us get there! In other words, you must be decisive about your intention.

3. The third strategy I would like to offer is to "chart your path." Quite honestly, I have had difficulty in times past with this one. I have found that I have not always been consistent. This means that it seemed like I would always have to start back at "square one" on a particular goal or an area of character development. If you

find that you have had challenges in this area too, then I have some good news. To chart your path, you will first have to refer to Strategy 2 above. If you know what you want to accomplish (intention), then you can begin to chart your path. One way you can do this is by journaling or keeping a small notebook handy, or using an app on your phone that allows for note taking, calendar scheduling, and reminders. Let me use an example of building a sandbox. If you want to build a sandbox for the neighborhood playground, and you have already set your intention, then you can begin to implement your plan by chunking it down one step at a time. For example, if you need to buy two by four planks, then one of the first steps you will need to take is to determine the size of the sandbox. The next step may be to purchase lumber or materials that you will use. Another step may be to determine the amount of sand you'll need. You get the picture, right? It's the same thing as "charting your path." You will not move greater than the effort you put into ridding yourself of hindrances that impede your progress. I have found it useful to set days, time limits, and completion dates on some of the most difficult tasks that I have had to do. You've got this! Try these three strategies, and watch how you can at least get your wheels spinning productively while you are *"HERE"*

The fact that you are still here is not by some serendipitous moment in time. You are here because you are supposed to be HERE. If I may do a play on words, then what I really mean is that you are here (alive), yes. But you are also *HERE* (where your circumstance has placed you) because of Divine order. Even if you have made choices less than godly, God has you here by Divine Design. "God's designs regarding you, and His methods of bringing about these designs, are infinitely wise." (Hahn, 2002) In cooperation with your choices (good or bad), the Divine brilliance of God has brought you to a place where He can do His most creative and restorative work in you.

You are here so that God can reveal more of Himself to you. *You are here* so that God can reveal more of His great plan for your life. He allowed you to come to this place of inquiry, uncertainty, and extreme conditions so that you can turn to Him for relational exchange and dependency, sustenance and trust. A.W. Tozer writes in his book, "The Pursuit of God, "God is a Person, and in the deep of His mighty nature, He thinks, wills, enjoys feels, loves, desires, and suffers as any other person may. In making Himself known to us, He stays by the familiar pattern of personality. He communicates with us through the avenues of our minds, our wills and our emotions…The continuous and unembarrassed interchange of love and thought between God and the soul…The intercourse between God and the soul is known to us in conscious personal awareness." (Tozer) So, you are HERE so that you can divinely blossom, grow, flourish, and thrive in conscious personal awareness that God is revealing Himself to you in a deeper, more intimate exchange of love, thought, and purpose.

You are here as a manifestation of intentional Divine thought. Surely as God created the world by the breath of His mouth, so He has intentionally created you by the work of His hands, by the thought of His mind, and by the image of His heart. Your life is a fulfillment of Divine Purpose. Being *here* is so much more than what you are supposed to be doing. Fulfilling your purpose is not always about what you are doing, but who you are becoming.

What Brings you HERE?
 Part Two

Who you are is more important to God than what you do. It is easy to become frustrated when you feel that you could be doing more about your circumstances, your purpose, or your life. It is at this place of frustration that God wants you to relax and hand over all of your concerns. Allow Him to navigate you through these difficulties. When you release your anxieties about everything coming together "right now", God uses this time to grow you.

During this growing process, He will meet you where you are and reveal to you why you are in the place to which you have arrived. If you are unclear, anxious, fearful, or have questions, ask Him anything. Philippians 4:6 states, "Be anxious for nothing, but in everything by prayer and supplication, with thanksgiving, let your requests be known to God; and the peace of God that passes all understanding will guard your heart and mind through Christ Jesus." God cares for you and wants you to be confident in His love.

You are here as a matter of the Divine expression of God's love. Love is the environment for which all things were created. Your being here has nothing to do with your family name, your profession, your status, your affluence, your bank account or any other material box that we limit ourselves in believing are essential to life. Rick Warren notes, "God created the entire universe. He created this planet; he created the human race. Then, He created you because He loves you. God created you as an object of His love. God made you so He could love you and so that you could love Him. God's love for you is the reason your heart is beating right now; it's the reason you're breathing." (Warren, Daily Hope with Rick W) (Warren, The Importance of Understanding God's Love, 2014)

God wants you to be a reflection of Himself (His character), so He avails himself to you three hundred and sixty-five days a year, seven days a week, twenty-four hours a day so that you can have access to His love, power, and direction. When God brings you to a place of brokenness, it is for the sole purpose of mending and molding you into His image. There's something absolutely remarkable about seeing yourself as a reflection of Divine Love. Take a mirror for example. When you look into a mirror, you see exactly who you are physically. Every detail of your facial and body features in the mirror are evident of who you are. But what about who you are on the inside? We all can use some spiritual sprucing up. By connecting with God in an intimate way, the Divine Spirit draws you closer to Him. The closer you become to the Creator, the more you begin to reflect His image, character, and nature. These beautiful qualities are hard to acquire unless you are in relationship with God. It's not about getting it all right. It's more about being alright in a right relationship with Him. He wants your nature to become more like His. So, how can you identify the nature of God? Some of His characteristics are kindness, merciful, thoughtful, gentle, forgiving, benevolent, tenderhearted, longsuffering, gracious, etc. are to name a few. Can you identify any areas of your life that can use a change? Taking on these characteristics is not easy so don't let it frustrate you when it becomes difficult. It takes time, and it takes prayer. You can pray and ask God to help you to desire these characteristics. You can ask Him to teach you how to implement this new way of being? Imagine how life inside and around you would change if you reflected a new Christ-centered nature. Here lies the starting pointing for living your true authentic divinely created purpose self.

Your being here also means several great things, such as realizing your purpose. You are here to impact the world around you with your greatness. That's right! You have greatness DNA. You cannot get around it. God has written a particular and unique code in your DNA that makes you unlike anyone or anything else in His creation. Your uniqueness is what He will use to speak to you, speak through you, and show you how He will use you to help others. Your purpose is not just about you. It is about others who God will place on your path throughout your lifetime. Your purpose will be realized when this mission is accomplished. If you are still trying to figure out what great impact you are making, then ask a few trusted friends and family members how you have impacted their life? You will see exactly what I am saying. Try it! Then come back to this chapter. Here are some basic questions you can ask; then record their responses on the lines provided below:

1. Have I ever been an encouragement to you? If so, in what way?

   _____

   _____

   _____

2. What do you see as some of my greatest strengths?

   _____

   _____

   _____

3. In what way have I impacted your life for better?

   _____

   _____

   _____

Now that you have recorded some of the responses from other people, you can clearly see that although you may not think so, you have added value to the lives of people. When you add value to people, you consequently give them hope.

Your being here also means that there is hope for someone else. People become more hopeful in their difficulties when they hear the stories of others who have overcome theirs. Your story must be told as a means of inspiration and encouragement. Even if you have yet to overcome, you have made it through to this point thus far. Tell that story!

Incidentally, I read recently in a devotional by Joyce Meyer about your *mess becoming your message*. Everyone has a story. Someone somewhere needs to hear your story so that they can rise above their challenges. Maybe you're thinking that you are in the midst of a challenge right now, so how can you help anyone else rise above their circumstance when you feel saddled by yours. Ok, let's say that you are. One of the sure ways to rise above your own personal challenge is by helping someone rise above theirs. Your being here is essential to the hope of mankind, which is a powerful tool that God uses to draw people to Him in love and partnership.

In this final segment, I would like for you to think of ways that you can make an impact on society or in your own community by sharing your story, or even your gifts. To get you started, listed are a few suggestions that will help you think about ways to get your story out so that you can make deposits into the lives of others:

1. People who live in homeless shelters could use some inspiration. Find out from the shelter's activities coordinator when you can come visit and speak with specific residents who will benefit from hearing an inspiring story. Write down at least 3 places you would like to contact

to share your story.

1._____2._____3_____

2. Meet up Groups: I just recently learned about Meet up groups. There is a group for just about anyone. Perhaps you can go online, www.meetup.com, and take a look at the various groups who have shared interests with you. You will be surprised at the number of groups in your community. You can share your story with them via social interactions. List them here:

1._____
2._____
3._____

3. Non-profit organizations, Boys and Girls Club, and community organizing groups are great places to sow into people. Your story can help restore trust, determination, hope, and genuine care in your community. List three community service groups you would like to join:

1._____
2._____
3._____

Your story is so unique that you have to share with

others how you've managed your life and how you have

overcome difficult obstacles. Maybe your story isn't a

glamorous one, but that doesn't matter because everyone you walk by may be facing some kind of battle. You will never know or understand the impact of telling your story. In the next chapter, I will share with you a segment of my story. In the meantime, look over your exercises. Think about some of your take-away(s) from reading this chapter. Share with a family member or friend any points that resonated with you.

Your take-away(s):

1._____
2._____
3._____
4._____

You are HERE because the gift of YOU is God's gift to Himself and to the world. You are also HERE because you have value. Anything of value is worth its existence to the person who *gave* it its value. You are HERE by way of Divine Intention. God wants you HERE!

Until we connect again in thought and vibes, make sure

you are always kind to yourself and others. I will meet you

in the next chapter. Peaceful blessings.

Chapter 2
RErooted

In the previous chapter, the entire emphasis was on why you are here. I have been where you are. Maybe the variables are slightly different, but the point is I had to go through the same process of recognizing, identifying, affirming, and using this time of uncertainty as teachable moments. I encouraged you to tell your story. If you would indulge me for a moment, I would like to share with you moments from my story.

When I was born, the world knew nothing about the great things God wanted to accomplish in my life. I doubt seriously if my parents even knew. Growing up for me was a series of self-discovery moments. I don't remember having my own individual thoughts until I was in high school. I think for the most part, I just said and did what was expected of me. Like us all, we come into this world unshaped and very moldable. We say, do speak, and repeat what we've been taught and shown until we are old enough to cognitively make sound decisions for ourselves. That moment was deferred for me because I never really thought I had a voice. I had lots of thoughts and ideas, but was too afraid to share them. I used to daydream about how life would be if only I had the chance to get out of my mind and step foot into this beautiful creative space I invented in my thoughts.

My thoughts eventually carried me away to a place where I could be as different as I wanted to be. But in reality, I really wasn't any different from any of my siblings, so I was told. All during adolescence, grade school, and high school, I pretty much felt very ordinary. I didn't particularly stand out in the crowd. I clearly wasn't the most popular girl at school. I wasn't the smartest kid in the class. I had friends, but was not a social butterfly as I had imagined I could be. But, as far back as I can remember, I have always been passionate about things. I poured my heart into whatever I found to do, especially with the arts. I loved to sing, dance, and involve myself in arts and crafts projects. I had become a true sensing person without realizing it. As a middle child, I grew to become quite observant. My most recurring observation was feeling as though I didn't fit within my family dynamics. I often felt unloved and ignored. I don't recall being affirmed that often. So, I lost myself in my own ability to create a safe place of acceptance.

Feeling accepted is a big deal to a child. As I grew older, the need to fit in increased. I think in some kind of strange way, it didn't matter anymore whether I fit in at home. What mattered was that I fit in at school among my peers. I recall an assignment I participated in when I was a tenth grader. I had to say a speech during a language arts class. I recited a parody of "Mary Had a Little Lamb," and the class roared with laughter and gave me a rousing applause. That was probably the first time I thought that I did something that people actually enjoyed. I felt accepted.

During the subsequent years of growth and development, I spent long hours of thought and contemplation about who I was. I think I've spent my entire life trying to figure out that mystery. However, it never really occurred to me that while I was trying to figure out everything in my head, a path had already been paved for me. Because I was unaware of my life's path, I spent too much time and a whole lot of energy trying live up to everyone's expectation. It was hard for me to differentiate between my true self and the person who I believed others wanted me to be. I'm not saying that people in my life put unrealistic expectations on me, but from where I was standing, I felt that there was an ideal that was taught to me, and I felt I was supposed to live up to that ideal. When I discovered that I actually had a voice and an opinion, I began to feel that I could bravely walk to the beat of my own drum.

The beat of my own drum became the tempo for which each rhythmic step of self-discovery would lead me on a path to exploring my purpose. I wish I could tell you that I have always known my path or purpose, but I can't. It was hard for me to even recognize that I had a path or a purpose because it was hard to recognize that I had any value. The truth is I have always struggled with feeling valued. The truth is I have always had challenges in knowing my worth. Consequently, I constantly gave away my worth, my value, my love, and my self-esteem for most of my adult life. I didn't realize how much of myself I was giving away. What I managed to keep were feelings of failure, rejection, disappointment, and abandonment that I buried deep in my soul.

I soon discovered that when someone is dealing with unresolved issues, or things that have been buried deep in their soul for most of their life, at some point, those issues will eventually come out. I know this to be true in my own life. There were times when these issues would surface and make an appearance in my insecurities. I certainly can recall a pattern of destructive behavior that started at age 18. By age 19, I gave birth to my only daughter. By the time I approached age 23, I had done anything and everything I was big and bad enough to do. But the good Lord intervened and subsequently led me to a Beauty School in which I enrolled (a rescue plan of the Father).

After I graduated and started working, my life seemed to detour on another route. I made some bad choices and poor judgment calls on major life decisions. I moved around a lot until I moved to Huntsville, Alabama in 1991. After several months, things went south in my marriage, so I was ready to go back home to Boston, but I chose to stay to make it work in Alabama.

I guess I had to make it work because I was tired of messing up. I really needed to find my niche in this new city. I started working at a local hair salon for 2 years. After two and a half years, I rented a booth at another salon. I wasn't satisfied working for other people, so I started my own salon in 1995. This was one of the most memorable times of my life. I fueled my passion for hair care and design, and I started a journey of being an entrepreneur. Although I have always loved being in the hair industry, it still never fully defined my purpose. If I had to pinpoint a time in my life when I felt my purpose was becoming clearer, I would probably pick age 37.

The revealing of my purpose became crystal clear in 2002. That year was one of the worst and best years of my life; things going on in my personal life being the worst. The best was seeing my daughter graduate from high school. In between the worst and the best days were lots of crying, loads of sadness, praying, journaling, going to school, serving in church, and many bouts of trying to understand what God had in mind for me to do.

I remember being in my closet, literally, on bended knees. I was crying out to God with an anguished soul asking him for relief from the hurt I was experiencing. As I wept, I heard a still small voice speak to my soul, "I am calling you." Then, I said, "Ok Lord, ok- ok Lord I hear you! Okay I accept the call that You have on my life." I had no idea what that meant, or how it was going to be manifested. Since then, I had to unlearn some truths that were imposed on me so that I could re-learn the truth that God has for me. It has taken many years of praying and pleading with God to help me feel like I was worth anything. Like many of you, as I've mentioned before, I have experienced failure, disappointments, sadness, rejection, and feeling alone. In the midst of all my troubles, God has kept His word that He would never leave me nor forsake me. He has been my comfort and guide.

The guidance that God has given me over these years has come by way of Providence, situations, people, opportunities, church fellowship, and spiritual development. The list goes on. How did I get from there to here? I can tell you that it has not been easy, but it has been doable. Your experience is also doable. It may not be comfortable or easy, but you can make it. If you are finding that your life has taken unexpected twists and turns and facing some difficult experiences, don't be discouraged. I have some hope for you.

Your hope starts with clearing out your mind first. Your mind can either be a weapon of mass destruction or an environment for renewal and creativity. Your mind is the sum total of your subconscious, past memories, and what you consciously take in on a daily basis. Even if your experiences have been some of the worst kind, they do not define your destiny. Even if people have spoken ill of you or over you, you cannot afford to believe this stuff anymore. God is ready to give you a paradigm shift. One of the ways He shifts you is by shifting your belief about Him and about yourself. God is capable of uprooting old patterns of thinking and faulty self-belief systems and replacing them with new structures He can nurture and grow. It may not happen overnight, but if you allow Him,

He will do a special work inside you. You must be patient even if it seems like nothing is changing.

The special work that God does is what I call root system work. So often, when we don't see things materializing on the surface, we defect to old patterns of thinking of believing that nothing is happening at all. These patterns occur beneath the surface of our soul (mind, body, and spirit). God does His most transformational work beneath the surface. Before we can get to a better place mentally, emotionally, physically, or spiritually, we have to allow God to renew the roots of our minds. More specifically, the roots that I am referring to are cycles of behavior and patterns of thinking that have become deterrents to our overall success. These roots are imbedded deeply in our sub-conscious. We don't have to put forth any effort to act on these impulses. The subconscious is like a never-ending recorder logging and projecting information.

We recall this information often times without thought as we experience the material world through our conscious decisions and choices. It's ok to ask God to uproot things that are no longer relevant to your current journey. I had to learn to allow God to re-root me so that He can re-route me. You have to allow God to re-root you so that He can re-route you. He takes the damaged roots of our past and grafts new roots into our mind so that He can re-route us on the path and purpose that He has declared and designed for you and me. This is one of the most arduous processes of all. Sometimes the process is painful. In my opinion, it is better to deal with the pain of transformation rather than the pain of mental and emotional incarceration. You have to be aware, awake, and present in this process so that when you find yourself repeating negative thoughts or untruths about yourself, you can allow God to re-root and re-route you through this process.

Recently, I went through another painful process of God re-rooting me. Some of the truths that I had accepted throughout my life that had ruptured my self-worth found a way to re-surface. Mind you, if something resurfaces, it usually means that there are still some roots that need to be pulled and replaced. God allowed me to go through a painful experience with a family member who had a history of mistreating me. Although, I had forgiven this person many times over, I could never understand why the mistreatment would happen over and over again. But God had already made Himself available way before the last incident happened. The year before, He warned me that He was going to take me to a deeper level of healing but I would have to experience a little more pain in order for the healing to be complete. Subsequently, He gave me the courage to speak up, and call the hurt by its rightful name. Although it was emotionally draining, I knew that God had brought me to a place where I had to trust Him for further healing. Just like hurt people hurt people? Healed people heal people. One of the hallmarks of Christian maturity is to extend genuine love and concern for a person who despises you. Let me tell you something: this was one of the most difficult challenges of my life because quite frankly, I would have preferred to dismiss everything. But God brought me to another level of healing by allowing me to face something so painful and grave. Needless to say, I am in a much better place. But He had to re-root me in order to re-route me.

In the process of being re-routed it is extremely difficult dealing with a dark season when nothing appears to be happening on the surface. The only thing that appeared to be happening on the surface was hardship. Prior to finishing this book, for almost five years, I had gone through a serious financial crisis. The business wasn't thriving, and I don't think I was trying to help it. I believe I had lost hope in my future dreams. I lost hope in the vision that God had given me for my up and coming business. The season of financial stillness was very real to me. There were times when trying to meet my monthly expenses became increasingly difficult. I cannot count how many times I faced eviction. There was not enough money coming in. I felt that if I abandoned my hope for building a new business, I would be stuck forever. Seemed like everything had minimal success. But just at the brink of everything falling apart, God would use someone to help me in my hour of greatest need. The last two of those five years, God took me on some amazing journeys of absolute surrender, absolute trust, and absolute dependence. The intimacy God and I now share matured during these dark days of what appeared to be no activity of God in moving me ahead in my personal life or the businesses. Now, I realize that God had been re-rooting me so that He can re-route me. I am still allowing God to lead me beside still waters as He restores my soul.

God will restore your soul as He continues the process of re-rooting you to re-route you. I want to make a few suggestions if you are in the midst of a dark lifeless season. At this point, I am hoping you realize that God is truly at work in your life. Please consider two critical steps in beginning to free yourself from your past, from being confined and bound to a mental world of un-truths.

1. **Your connectedness with God is paramount to your freedom**. Your freedom includes mental, emotional, physical, and spiritual release. Your connectedness with God will help you see your

value. Renowned Author and Leadership Development Expert, John Maxwell states, "You must see value in yourself to add value to yourself." The Scriptures also speak on this topic of value: I Peter 2:9 reads, "But you are a chosen race, a royal priesthood, a holy nation, a people for his own possession, that you may proclaim the excellencies of him who called you out of darkness into his marvelous light." ESV. It is so essential that you remain connected to God. For in Him is Light. He will be Light to the very dark places of your life which will begin to liberate your mind. There are many ways to stay connected to God. But first you have to realize that God created mankind to be involved in the lives of all people. He created you for Himself. You, who are of God, are not completely connected until you are truly, unreservedly, unconditionally in God. Allow God full permission to do His perfect work in you.

2.   **The second step I would like to suggest is to allow God to weed out things that are draining you of your life force**. You have been on this journey for a very long time. You have accumulated quite a few weeds. We all have some of what is considered proverbial "weeds." I don't think I have to go in detail about the weeds to which I am referring. But just in case, you may have missed a weed or two, please do not disqualify envy, jealousy, divisiveness, un-forgiveness, hatred, lack of boundaries, cynicism, criticism, and the list goes on. It is super important to let God be a weed killer of this stuff. Get it out from around your house (your heart)! You may have to seek counseling from

a professional, clergy, counselor, or life coach. You will free yourself the moment you decide that you will no longer allow weeds to deplete all the nutrients that healthy thoughts and behaviors need. Weeds take away from the value of the beautiful plant or flower that is growing. Weeds can mimic healthy foliage. So God has to do this work in you. In my opinion, it is next to impossible to access your true authentic self with weeds blocking the way. You must begin the process of allowing God to kill the accumulation of your emotional weeds, rejection weeds, fear weeds, weeds of hurt and abuse, and any other weeds that have taken over. These weeds mimic voices. Those voices remind you that *you have become the weeds to which you need to rid yourself.* You are *not* useless weeds. When there is this type of non-productive clutter growing in your mind, it manifests into walls of weeds; a big long wall of weeds that have the length and width of the Great Wall of China. You won't let yourself out beyond the wall, and you won't let anyone within the wall. This wall of weeds that you have built has specific characteristics that identify you as the soil for which these weeds have taken up residence. They bury themselves deep within so that they are toxic, sensitive, condescending, cynical, short-tempered, impatient, depressed, or even paranoid. This is *not* who you are. I realize that after having had bad experiences or a change in life events, anyone can become a hostage to their hostility. Refuse to allow these weeds to define you. It is time to let God get His divine weed killer and uproot them. And in their place, He will give you new roots of character so that you are no longer bound by limited potential. Your potential will begin to give rise to producing beauty instead of ashes. If you start with the assignments that I have shared with you, you will begin to open a whole new world for yourself and others as you are being re-rooted to be re-routed.

Chapter 3
Dark and Dormant

What is so significant about the tulip bulb in the Fall Season? Glad you are thinking about that question. The tulip bulb has so many characteristics. But this chapter is not so much about the uniqueness of the tulip bulb, inasmuch as the Season in which it is planted. This chapter is about the Fall Season. As you have read in the Introduction, the tulip bulb is typically planted in the Fall Season for a reason. "Bulbs are specialized underground plant parts that store food for the plant. Most bulb-type plants are herbaceous perennials in which the shoots die down at the end of a growing season, and the plant survives in the ground as a dormant, fleshy organ that bears buds to produce new shoots for the next season. These plants are well suited to withstanding periods of adverse growing conditions in their yearly growing cycle." (What's In a Name?, 2014)

Just like tulips, you may be feeling like you're going through a fall season for some unknown reason. I'm not sure why, but the least we can do is take a look at some of the characteristics of the fall season as it relates to tulips. The fall season is conducive for planting bulbs. It is an ideal time to get them in the ground before the extremely cold weather comes and freezes the surface of the ground.

Master Gardner and About.com Blog writer, Marie Iannotti explains why you should plant your tulip bulb in the fall before the ground freezes, *"Once the ground has frozen and you can no longer dig, you might be tempted to toss your bulbs into a dark corner of the basement and forget about them until spring. But spring blooming bulbs are not like dahlias, gladioli or other summer blooming tender bulbs that can be stored away for winter. Remember they need to grow some roots and experience a period of chilling, to sprout next season. They only have enough energy stored to get them through one dormant season. They need to grow next year to replenish themselves."* (Ionatti, 2014)

Just as the fall season is prime time to plant tulip bulbs, your fall season is necessary and critical for your spring season. In other words, you may feel like nothing is happening in your life. You may feel that you are frozen in time. You may think about tossing yourself into some dark corner of your world and just be forgotten about; to the contrary my friend. During this seemingly chilling time of your life, God has prepared for you a ground in which He has divinely dug up for you. Although it may be unbeknownst to you, He is establishing your roots, causing them to grow in ways that will establish you for the next sprouting moment. It is in this season that your trust in God is just enough energy source, and is sufficient to get you through right now. The trust you have now will become paramount to the trust you will need as He brings you through from being dormant to a season of flourishing and replenishing.

A season of flourishing and replenishing do not happen all of a sudden. When spring finally arrives, we watch the transition of the trees, grass, flowers, and other foliage emerge with all the possibility and potential of NEW creations. Watching God's budding creation arouses a joyful hope and expectation of the days ahead that will bring awesome sunshine, great weather, delightful food, outdoor activities, family gatherings, seasonal sports, with so many other particulars that are relative to the change of weather conditions. Likewise, your season of flourishing and replenishing won't happen all of a sudden. Your spring season will certainly arrive. But, you have to realize that your transition is a process in progress. As you emerge from dormancy to alive and thriving, all the inner workings of your mind, body, and spirit during your fall season will begin to manifest into all the possibility and potential of a NEW creation that the Creator has established in you from the beginning. You will emerge into a life of exceeding abundantly-- more than you can think or ask. See Ephesians 3:20.

When I think about my season of exceeding abundantly, it would not have happened had it not been for my fall season of preparation. My fall season seemed so, so, so long. It seemed as though I would never see the light of day. There were many times I just wanted to give up. I was still praying and still trusting. Most days were bright, but there were some dark days too. Satan knows when you are having dark days. He uses those opportunities to get you to distrust God and lean unto your own understanding. There were many instances when I leaned unto my own understanding, and all that did was make things more complicated by getting myself in trouble. Most of the trouble I created. It had everything to do with my lack of being fully committed in obeying God. I made excuses, bargained, and justified what I thought was okay to do. Until one day it seemed like the bottom fell out. I didn't see this trial coming; but because I wasn't walking in full obedience, God allowed it to take place. I was not listening to God until He made it crystal clear that I had better listen or I would find myself in a situation that would tear me away from Him. Needless to say, I was devastated. This experience only exacerbated an already existing fall season for me. During this time, it finally dawned on me, or should I say, I finally started listening to God more intently. I wasn't sure how long the trials were going to last, but I finally decided that I was going to outlast my trials by the grace of God.

What God did for me during my darkest days was unbelievable and very characteristic of God. I must admit that had I been obedient and totally surrendered and committed to God in the first place, He probably would have given me another course to follow. But because I wanted to do things my way, and decided to compromise my commitment to the Lord, He allowed me to crash right into the very decisions I thought were going to turn out right for me. The crazy thing is my relationship with the Lord has grown exponentially over the past 25 years or more. I can look back over my life and see exactly how God had matured me spiritually. But there were some areas of my heart that were not fully surrendered. I did not know they weren't surrendered, but God knew, and when the tests or temptation came unsuspectedly, I failed. Here I am fully committed to the Lord (so I thought), but I failed at passing some of the simplest tests. Sometimes, we try to hold on to what we cherish or love and try to make God cosign on our foolishness. God is not going to give His stamp of approval on anything that is a departure from His Word. He knows what is best for us and for what purpose He created us. The one thing that God will not make us do is surrender and give Him our heart completely. We have to decide that our relationship with God will always trump any relationship to anything or anybody. Our relationship with the Master has to be our number one relationship in our life.

Once, the bottom fell out, I remember the Holy Spirit speaking to me and saying that there would be difficult days ahead, but He was going to carry and sustain me. I covenanted with God that I was going to do things His way. It was in that moment that I knew that my way of doing things had not worked for me. I made up in my mind that since it was not working for me, I was going to do things God's way. The Holy Spirit led me to books, materials, and lessons that begin to shape how intimately God wanted us to become in relationship. Through my readings and studying, it was clear that I had to absolutely surrender, absolutely, trust, absolutely abide in Him, and absolutely yield. Once I asked the Lord to teach me how to position myself to be at these places of absolutes, He began to lead me, guide me, and teach me what is important to Him. And this time, I listened.

Listening to God is going to be the number one thing you are going to have to do in this dark, cold, and lifeless fall season. Just like the tulip bulb is planted in the fall in preparation of budding and blossoming in the spring, so it is with you. Your preparation in this fall season of your life is paramount to your spring season-- the one to which you are heading. The moment you decide that you are giving God your entire all, He will take all that you have currently, and give you all that He has for you divinely. I believe that. But in the meantime, you have some work that you need to do in preparation of God working on your behalf.

I would like for you to put into practice three things as your prepare for your new season.

1. **Partner with God in prayer**. Since you know that God is still working through chilling cold seasons when things seem to be inactive, why not

work with Him instead of resisting what is happening in your life? When you welcome all that is coming to you right now, you make room for the difficulty to pass through, and for the growth to reshape your thoughts, your plans, and your future. Partnering with Him means that you will spend intimate time with Him in prayer, in praise, and in His Word. You must stay connected to Him at all times. By so doing, He will convey to you as well as confirm what He is doing and where He is leading you.

2. **Give voice to that which you would like to see become manifest in your life.** Speak a word of declaration to yourself in agreement with what God is doing. Repeat this declaration every day, *"I declare that God is bringing about new seasons of growth. I will not get stagnant and*

hold on to the old. I will be open to change

knowing that God has something better in front

of me. New doors of opportunity, new

relationships, and new levels of favor are in my

future. This is my declaration." Joel Osteen.

3. **Take a shower**. Actually, I am using a shower

for imagery purposes. Let me explain the

symbolism right now. When you take a shower,

what is the first thing that you do? Typically, you

stand in the shower and allow your entire body to

get wet. Then, you begin to lather with soap or

body wash. You lather everything, trying to not

to miss any part of the cleaning process. Then

you rinse off, and maybe lather once or twice

more, then rinse. Finally, you prepare to get out

of the shower by starting the drying process.

Most people will grab a towel and dry off. Your

shower will now take on a new meaning. Every time you stand under the shower head to get wet, think about God causing rain to sprinkle on you until you are fully wet and immersed in Him. Lathering up now becomes your symbol for God scrubbing and cleaning from your life any and every thing that hinders you from flourishing. This includes cleaning up your past, your failures, your disappointments, your negative thinking, procrastination, self-doubt, and any other degree of limiting beliefs. Drying off is your *cue* for getting prepared. As you dry off, you know the next thing you will be doing is putting on clothes and getting ready for what's next on your agenda. Drying off for you now becomes a mindset of preparation, expectation, and manifestation. God prepares you to position you, prosper you, and pronounce to you His plan of goodness that He has in store for your future. See *Jeremiah 29:11.*

The reason why it is important for you to know and understand why God prepares you is so that you may understand that everything that God has purposed for you is intentional. This season of preparation involves more than just a readiness phase. If you would think about it for a moment, I am sure you can recall that any time in your past when you had to prepare for something, it nearly took everything you had inside to pull it all together. Even something as simple as preparing to take a trip involves so much planning. May I remind you that you are indeed planning for a trip: your heavenly home! So don't be surprised if this stage of preparation nearly takes you out. Seriously though, all along the way to heaven you are going to encounter changes, obstacles, setbacks, mood swings, indecisiveness, being adamant and sure.

Sometimes, you may even experience a sense of *being stagnant*. We call these the variables of life. But just because life happens, doesn't mean that you will not experience the fullness of God's promises and purposes for your life.

Your life may seem like it is in a tailspin right now. Maybe you are not experiencing the abundant life that Jesus promised you. Sometimes it seems like God has forgotten you. I certainly know what that feels like. I remember in 2013 crying out before God to transition me out of Huntsville. I begged and cried. I even accused Him of forgetting about me and not wanting me to have the things for which I had been praying. I asked Him on so many occasions why He wasn't helping me. One day, I just got tired of asking, so I stopped. Once I stopped all of this melodrama with God, He was able to give me the comfort of His Presence and the assurance of His Word. There's a lot to be said about the peace of God. Sometimes, God will not change your circumstances, but He will change you. I am a living witness that God will give you peace in your season of preparation.

Preparation can be something difficult to handle. When a person decides that he or she will plant a garden, the very first thing is to get the soil ready. If the ground has never been planted upon, then the ground has to be broken up, tilled, de-rocked, softened, fertilized, etc. So it is with our lives. When God begins to prepare us for His purposes, we must allow Him to break up the stony places in our hearts, till up some bad habits, de-rock some poor and faulty thinking, soften our rough edges, and fertilize us with His Holy Spirit.

The Holy Spirit knows the mind of God. He already knows why you and I were created and for what purpose we were created. His job is to reveal to us, in perfect timing, that which God has already put in order for us. In other words, your life's purpose has already been laid out even before you were created. If you feel that God has not revealed to you His great plan for your life, I am willing to bet that it is because He is still preparing you.

While God is preparing you, you must learn to cultivate patience in the preparation. Godly patience has become so irrelevant these days. Patiently waiting on God can try your faith in every inconceivable direction. Patience in the preparation calls for standing firm on who God is and what He says. It is extremely difficult to do in the natural realm, especially in light of long periods of time waiting for God to answer. But it is very doable in the spiritual realm because God's Spirit is at work within us. While waiting patiently upon God, we can become disgruntled, unhappy, impatient, etc., but we have to learn how to allow our souls to be satisfied with His goodness while we wait. The moment God sees that your soul is ready and satisfied with Him, He will give you clear directives as to what direction, action, and or initiative you need to take to get things moving for you. When God sees that you are ready to know His will, He will also equip you to do His will. Listed are a few steps you can take while you are allowing God to prepare you.

1. **Prepare and be aware**. The Bible instructs us to be sober. This means pay attention, be aware. The enemy is stealthy in that he will attempt to distract you. Your responsibility is to listen to God. In most cases, God speaks to us in a still small voice. If you are listening to every other voice, you will not hear God's. Chances are God is whispering to you what He wants you to know or an action He wants you to take. You will not be able to differentiate between the voice of the enemy and God's if you allow too many distractions to deafen you. Being aware also means that you value time. When God is preparing you, He also wants you to make time to commune with Him. You must set aside some quiet time

with God and be still. Many times, when we are waiting for an answer from God, we can squander away time and energy. Be certain to stay in unbroken communion with God.

2. **Explore new ways to use your talents and gifts**. You would be surprised to find people, places, and events that cater to things that may interest you. I have discovered that when I step outside my realm of familiarity, something creative rises up in me. God's resources are inexhaustible. He will continue to pour into you and carve new and creative ways for you to enjoy life. I know this from experience. God breathed new life in me in my darkest moments. Some of the things that I did included a couple of triathlons, bike races, concert parks, hiking, and most recently, art journaling. God will do the same for you. When God's creativity flows through you, He will birth new and refreshing creative opportunities for you to thrive-- not merely survive.

3. A phrase that Andy Dufregne spoke in the movie, *Shawshank Redemption* was **"Get busy living or get busy dying."** What are you busy doing? Living or dying? Perish the thought if you are slowly dying because you don't see any movement in your life. Start by

writing down some life goals. I have mine posted on the wall. By so doing, you have a daily reminder of things that you would like to accomplish or ways in which you would like to develop. If you have already written down your life goals, then take them before God and ask Him to show you how these goals may materialize, how they benefit others, and how they may meet His approval. Living God's best life for you has nothing to do with what you do or do not have. It does, however, have everything to do with your affiliation, attachment, relationship, commitment, and honor you have with and for the Lifegiver. Jesus came to give life. If He has already given you life, then you should be living a life exemplary of that vitality.

By taking these steps, you are actually generating new cell activity in your brain. When your brain processes new information, it creates new cells. New cells can only mean new life: Regeneration. You're on your way from transitioning from a place of cold chilling darkness to a place of surface breaking emergence.

Chapter 4
Cracks In the Ground!

Since we've been doing a lot of talking about tulips and drawing comparisons with our lives and the growth span of tulip bulbs, let's take a look at what happens after the planting of the bulbs. In the previous chapters, we discussed the preparation process as it relates to the ground being prepared and our lives being prepared. Let us say that the bulbs have already been planted, the dormant season or fall season has come and is now on its way out. Now, all we're waiting to see is the emergence of the flower as it processes through its respective stages.

The ground-breaking, ground-cracking stage is probably one of the most pivotal of all stages because it denotes a change, a turn-around: something revolutionary preparing to happen. When I think of this stage, one word comes to mind – emerge! All the activity that has taken place in the former season will manifest itself as fruit in the latter season. This stage reminds me of Job 8:7 which speaks to us that though our former season was small yet our latter season will greatly increase.

The root activity beneath the surface that seemed so dormant and void of beauty never stopped working. Production was going on all along. So it is with your life. In your season of inactivity, the Master Gardner Himself has still been moving things right along. This is your cue to "shout" right now. Don't ever confuse motion with movement. As my pastor explained one day, you can be in motion but have no movement. You can also be in movement without being in motion.

Let me explain. Your season of distress, discomfort, despair or desperation has been moving you to this point of ground-breaking emergence. You were in movement although you were not necessarily in motion. Now take one of your contemporaries with whom you may share similar skill sets. It seems as though everything is working out in his or her favor because you see them in motion. But what you don't know is that because you see them in motion doesn't necessarily mean that they've been moved higher or upward. Motion is just activity by itself. Movement is a succession of activity that leads to a destination. See your destination has always been set for you, but you didn't know it because you kept confusing your lack of motion with your God-sanctioned movement.

I know first-hand what it means to get movement and motion confused. See, I have not necessarily been in motion in one main area that is very important to me; my business, Presence with Purpose. It is my recent business birth child. Well, I have been giving birth to this business for the past five years. I still cannot seem to get good steady footing. In other words, it seemed as though I was hitting and missing at keeping this thing moving consistently. It seemed that I would have extreme highs in terms of motivation, creativity, and marketing. But, then I would experience equally distressful lows, meaning very little to no activity at all. Even my creativity seemed so stifled. I couldn't think, plan, or stick with anything substantive that would garner interest or income. I basically lost faith in what I could offer in this new emerging industry.

What I did not factor in (but now realize) is that although I had not been in motion, I had been in movement. God needed me to be just where I was, completely depending on Him. God is a Genius when it comes to movement and timing.

During the past two years, I have re-committed my entire life to God on a level such as never before. Since making that commitment, I have had a series of tests that have kept me on my knees. At the same time, I was growing in grace as I began to dig deep in books that strengthened my faith and taught me more about the will and compassion that God has for me.

There were several key directives that God gave me: abide, yield, surrender, wait, and trust. I dare to say that these areas of complete dependence on God were stretching me beyond belief. I knew that if I were to see the full manifestation of God's power and authority in my life, I had to allow Him to position me exactly where He wanted.

Do you know where God wants you to be? Let me help you out? God wants you to be so in love with Him that you are willing to abide in Him, yield to His will, surrender your complete self to Him, wait patiently on Him, and trust Him with all of your heart. Please let me alert you that it is impossible to get to this place all by yourself. You will need the agency of the Holy Spirit along with a decisive will to please God. You are probably wondering how long it will take, and whether or not you will have to arrive with these attributes before God says "yes. " Allow me to explain that God has already answered your prayer. He may not have revealed the answer to you yet because you are not ready. He is actually waiting on you while you think you are waiting on Him. Your main objective at this point is to wait "in" Him and not necessarily on Him.

Waiting for something that you've been praying for can be a very daunting process. What you must keep in mind is that your waiting is not in vain. You must also keep in mind that your waiting is also necessary. If God would allow you to emerge and pierce through your dark season prematurely, you would bypass a very critical step in faith development. It is one thing to declare one's faith when things are going relatively well. It's a whole different scenario and faith muscles involved when you have to stay engaged in your faith when there appears to be no sign of your breakthrough.

When a plant breaks through the ground during spring, we typically notice the little shoots; but before long, many of us will soon forget about the little shoot. The memory of the tiny shoot is soon forgotten because the rapid growth rate of the plant is soon realized when the flower is in full bloom.

Please do not hurry God. He knows what He is doing. Even as I am typing this sentence, I am sensing that I am speaking to myself as well. But you know, it is a good feeling to wait on God, and learning to be okay with that.

Great faith is built by one trial at a time, even in the face of what seems like apparent failure. Rest assured--failure is not what God has in mind for you. What He actually has in mind for you is a plan. Jeremiah 29:11 (MSG) speaks to this truth. It states, "I know what I'm doing. I have it all planned out—plans to take care of you, not abandon you, plans to give you the future you hope for."

The waiting process is set up for you to actually believe what God has promised. If you are fretting about God's intention for you, then you are still not ready for Him to manifest His promise to you. Bear in mind that His promises are sure to come to pass. Check out what 2 Corinthians 1:20 (KJV) declares, "For all the promises of God in him are yea, and in him Amen, unto the glory of God by us." So, I'm thinking that if God has plans for you and me, and all of His promises are yes and amen, then we can be assured that our future is secure in Him who has declared it to be. Thank you Jesus! The heavenly Father really wants you to take Him at His word. "Jesus said unto him, if thou canst believe, all things *are* possible to him that believeth." Mark 9:23

Believing that God has your best interest at heart will also catapult you forward in faith. You are getting ready to crack through the ground of your circumstance. Don't be afraid of the crack in the ground. It is called a BREAKTHROUGH! What may seem like an eruption in your life may actually be your breaking forth in the fullness of the promise God has given you. Remain in Him. Stay in His will. Keep your faith in the Father. Because God's word is so sure, it will do you well to stay in an attitude of expectancy. The farmer knows that as long as he plants and waters his crops, he can expect a harvest. Are you expecting a harvest? I surely hope so! Isaiah 61:5 makes it very clear, "My soul, wait thou only upon God;

for my expectation is from him." Why not? Is He not

Omnipotent?

Three most important things to do while waiting for a breakthrough:

1. **Pray**! I am sure you are already doing that. But if not, begin praying to God. If you are, then pray some more. God is interested in having communication with you. He wants to talk to you and He wants you to want to talk to Him. If you are having a hard time making time for daily prayer, then today is a great day to start. You don't have to be formal. You don't have to worry about saying all the right words. Just speak from your heart.

2. **Prepare**! Start preparing for your breakthrough before your breakthrough. A simple prayer asking God for guidance on how you should prepare. For example: If you are waiting for God to send you that special someone with whom you will spend your life, then you should be expecting God to answer every day. Make sure you are emotional, spiritually, physically, and financially prepared. Remember that your break through is already on the horizon... It's not only in your words, it's in your actions. If you really believe God is going to do just what He says, then begin walking in faith. Put everything in order.

3. **Serve**! Yes, I said it. There are so many people worse off than you. There are many people in your surrounding area who would love to hear a

85

word from the Lord through you. One way to begin serving is through volunteering. Volunteering will change your life. Service to others is a self-less act of kindness. God gives us gifts so that we can gift others. There are many organizations and agencies that could use your support. Please give it some serious thought about how you would like to give back to your community. The reason why service is so important is because helping others is a reflection of Christ's character. God is looking for people who have a heart of compassion to serve.

As I am reflecting on earlier times in my acquiescing to God's direction for my life, I am reminded as far back as I can remember, that I have generally been an artsy person. I tend to be that person who grabs everything I can possibly get from life experiences, whether it is music, theater, close relationships, nature, volunteering, or adventure and fun. Equally, I have always been a lover of good words, great phrases, and awesome quotes. Often times, I would read or hear something very profound, or even would make a statement, then muse over it. It wouldn't be long before I couldn't wait to share what was given to me by way of inspiration with other people. I know God has given me a voice. He has given me a presence with people.

He has given me a presence with purpose. On that note, may I add, that I am the owner of Presence with Purpose Center for Inner Healing and Personal Growth. I am a certified licensed personal growth and productivity coach. I help people become better at what they do by helping them to become the best at who they are. I accomplish this through training and development workshops, workplace seminars, private coaching, speaking engagements, conferences, and life coaching.

I remember when I started this business. To be honest with you, I said to myself on a number of occasions what I was not going to do. One of the things I thought I was NOT going to do was pro bono work. I felt as though I had put in my time with the other business for over 24 years. I figured I had done my share of elbow grease work. Therefore, I felt as though I was deserving of getting paid every time I performed a service. Well, little did I know, God had another plan. I began to volunteer for a home for teen mothers. I volunteered for a local hospice agency. I am a servant. My job is serving. Whenever I was asked to speak to someone in a vicarious situation, it was no longer about getting paid. It was about serving, about helping. Just recently, I was listening to an audio recording about success. One specific statement that the author shared was that if an individual really wanted to move forward in success, they need to begin doing what they love. He further suggested that they shouldn't be concerned about money right away.

Whatever it is that you want to do, then begin doing it today. If you want to write a book, start today. If you want to run a marathon, begin training today. If you want to own a business, put together a business plan today. Whatever it may be, you must rise to action. Give it a try, and watch the doors begin to open. Give it a try, and watch God begin to crack open supernatural opportunities that you would have never expected.

Chapter 5
Shoot! What is this?

It's kind of funny to watch bulbs bloom in the spring. In my region, the tulip usually starts to peak through the ground after the daffodils. At first the only visible part of the tulip plant is the green tip. Who really pays any attention to a little green tip sticking up through the ground? Not many people notice something so small unless they planted the bulb themselves. The little green tip is called a shoot. The shoot is the first visible sign of emergence. It's kind of hard to determine the rate of progress by the shoot, but actually the breakthrough of the "shoot" is the fastest phase of them all. The beauty of observing this growth cycle is that ordinarily, the growing process goes unnoticed until one day the actual tulip appears above the ground in what seems like out of nowhere. Let me stop right there.

I want to draw a very simple comparison. Much like the little green tip of the tulip of which hardly no one ever pays attention to (except the *Gardner*), your progress may seem to go unnoticed by everyone around you, except the Gardner. You do know who the Master Gardner is, don't you? See, often times progress is so incremental that the person making the progress may not even see it, and in despair, may be tempted to give up. But God is the one who planted you where you are. It is not for anyone to undermine the progress of your process. Not even you!

Do you remember the Creation story found in the book of Genesis? Remember how God spoke and created all living life? Genesis 1:11-12 describes God's creative work, "Then he commanded, "Let the earth produce all kinds of plants, those that bear grain and those that bear fruit"—and it was done. So the earth produced all kinds of plants, and God was pleased with what he saw."

And God was pleased with what he saw! When God looks at you as his creation, he has already declared that His creating you was good work. And of course we are familiar with the text that assures us that the good work God started in us, He is faithful to complete until Jesus returns (Philippians 1:6). If God has your long range plans already in motion and movement, surely you've got to know that He has the journey to your completion already mapped out.

From the time you were conceived, God had a plan for your life. You are not here by the decisions of two people per se, but you are here because God created you to love you, to provide for you, to protect you, to establish you, to bring to you an inheritance. In your darkest hour, you must always remember that the dream that God has placed in your heart is a part of the purposes He has called you to live out. There is no possible way that God would leave you incapacitated to fulfill your God-given purpose.

Speaking of purposes, the tulip plants and other flowering foliage are to beautify the earth and provide viable oxygen exchange to the earth. So, in essence, when the tulip has pierced through the ground, it then begins a process of growing to full maturation in order to provide the maximum benefit to the gardener and to those who would enjoy the array of beauty it beholds.

The sooner you welcome your season of growth, the more pliable you will become in the hands of the Master Gardner. The tulip doesn't argue against nature. It doesn't rebel against its genetic makeup. It doesn't try to be anything else but a tulip. It can't because it does what the Creator tells it. So it is with you: make sure that you work in harmony with nature. Be certain that you live out your divine genetic makeup. Purpose in your heart that you will not be anyone other than your genuine authentic self. How can you be anyone else? You can't! Your growth in this season is different from any other transitional growth. How do I know this? Because you are reading this book. People who are transitioning want to know what to expect. They typically want to know what type of adjustments they will need to make. They often times want to know what's new on the horizon. That's how I know. Furthermore, I am that person! You can laugh here. It's ok.

It's ok to recognize a need for growth and change. Pity the person who is okay with being the same person in the same way all the time. I know you're not that person. But at any rate, growth and change are synonymous with transition. While you are transitioning, you may feel a little stretched in many ways. You may have had difficult experiences, maybe even a change in life events. I have found that whenever a person is recognizing a need to transition, it is precipitated by a change in circumstances, perhaps a change in life's perspective.

I have spoken to many people about a little nudging or even discontent that they are experiencing. Sometimes, what follows next is, "something's got to change!" I so remember those feelings. Have you? I remember feeling restless, hopeless, frustrated, and plain ol' tired of being where I was at the time.

In an earlier chapter, I explained how much I cried out to God to transition me location-wise. I begged Him to please let me go and work somewhere else. However, God did not transition me. He kept me right where I was. Little did I know, I was not prepared to move. While I contended with God that I had done all I could do in Huntsville, He promptly let me know that He was not finished doing what

He needed to do in me. Wow! Even as I am typing this sentence, I am amazed at the work that God is actually doing inside of me.

Let me say right here and right now that I am grateful. Had God moved me when I insisted, I can tell you right now that I would probably be in the worst possible condition on all levels. God is in control of the progress that He needs to make in our lives. We are the ones who continue to hold Him up. We whine, we throw temper tantrums, we rebel, and we often times become very stubborn. But because He is faithful to complete what He started in us, He is mega-patient with us. Well, at least I can speak for myself.

The growing process can weaken or strengthen your faith. If a person decides that he or she would rather succumb to being overwhelmed by his or her circumstances, the progression of faith is weakened. The faith process progresses and is strengthened when an individual decides that in spite of his or her circumstances, he or she will take God at His word. The faith process is deterred when an individual fails to believe and allows doubt to overshadow what God says in His word. Let's take a look at what the Bible says about the lack of faith in Matthew 14:31, "Immediately Jesus reached out his hand and caught him. "You of little faith", he said, "why did you doubt?"" Jesus was speaking to Peter in this passage.

I'm sure you are familiar with this story of Peter walking on water. Bear in mind though, prior to this feat, Peter had just witnessed a mighty miracle of God when Jesus had just fed five thousand people. With a recent experience right behind him, and Jesus right before him, Peter still doubted. Christ checked him on it because he should have had more faith in Jesus. Needless to say, Peter still had some growing to do.

Later on in the New Testament we see that Peter really "flaked out" on Jesus by denying him. Poor Peter-- he just couldn't keep it together-- you know, the faith thing. The faith thing is what helps us to grow. You may be in a Peter-like situation where you are doubting God. You have seen Him do many miracles in the past. You have exercised great faith many times before when you have found yourself in very precarious situations. Yet, while you realize all of this, you continue to find yourself questioning whether God is going to reach out and take you by the hand and bring you to safety or a better place in your circumstances.

In order for you to grow to great faith, these trials you are facing in your season of growth will draw you closer to God if you will allow them. Trials are very necessary. God uses trials to get our attention, to help us to recognize and acknowledge His Sovereign will, and draw us closer to Him intimately. God knows what we need before we ask. Better yet, He knows what we need even if we never ask. I love that God takes the initiative and exercises His prerogative to do the drawing. Your growth to great season is paramount to your flourishing season. When have you ever seen anything flourish before it started growing? Exactly! Never! You've got to grow into shoots *now* in order to get to the beauty of the blossom *later*! God bless you!

Chapter 6
Waiting to Blossom

Steve Maraboli nailed it when he made the above quote. It is quite frustrating when you are waiting to bloom, and the conditions are not yet ready for that phase. Reminds me of a lingering winter season that just won't go away. Have you been feeling like you've been in a never-ending winter season? When winter has overstayed its welcome, people begin to get a little tired of sweaters, coats, layers of clothes, and winter gloom. Nothing is more frustrating than for the cold months of winter to hang around as though there is not another season on the horizon.

In my region, we have short winters. By March, we would like to think that most of the cold weather is saying "farewell." The sun begins to shine longer, grass begins to grow, birds are finding their way back to familiar territory, leaves begin to turn green, etc. Then all of a sudden, we get a cold spell. Unbelievable! Then we have to pull out warm clothes again until the cold passes. Life can be quite like that sometimes. Many people have experienced a very long winter of trials, challenges, lack, disappointments, and maybe even loss.

Just when it seems that the load of the heaviness has lifted, there comes another issue that sets them back. Have you ever experienced a time in your life when a series of bad things was happening, then you finally got a break? Just as soon as circumstances began to look better, a wave of challenges knocked you down? It would be nice that once we get over one problem, we would get a long break before another problem rears its ugly head.

Well, there is some good news in this. Just as seasons do not last forever, neither do problems. Thank God for the change of seasons. Even if winter lasts longer than anticipated, it will eventually fade into spring. In the meantime, and in between time of your winter and spring transition, is what I want to call the "waiting it out" period. This period is probably one of the most difficult periods of all life transitions. It's almost parallel to the old saying, "the light at the end of the tunnel." But sometimes it seems that the closer you get to the light the farther away it appears. To draw a correlation, the closer you get to your breakthrough, the longer it seems for it to materialize.

As I stated before, the harshness of winter does not last always. The "waiting it out period" is very necessary. Right before the tulip tip breaks through the surface of the ground, everything sufficient for its survival has been prepared. All the nutrients from the soil is provided to sustain it above ground.

Are you ready to be above ground? I am sure you are, and so am I. The "waiting period" is so significant to your blossom season that the good Lord factored and worked it into your journey. There are a few things you need to know about waiting on God. If anyone knows about waiting on God, it sure is me. In my season of waiting, I became a student of Christ's discipleship school. The school where you learn the discipline of waiting or patience. It took a near catastrophe for me to finally realize that God's way is the right and only way; and if I were to see the manifestation of His power in my life, I had better start listening, and waiting for Him to move.

The most important thing I would like to share with you is that waiting on God is a virtue. The waiting on Him entails so much that I really don't have the space to write it all. However, I want to share with you what I've learned about waiting on God. Let's start with, you were also created to wait on God. In this statement, the word *wait* can be interpreted as dependence on God. There is a scriptural reference to back this up: Psalm 104:27-28… "These wait all upon thee; that thou mayest give them their meat in due season. That thou givest them they gather: thou openest thine hand, they are filled with good." All of creation waits on God. Everything about nature is dependent upon God and His provisions; including you and me. Somehow, we have mistakenly turned waiting on God a drudgery. Waiting on God and depending on Him should be man's highest joy. Andrew Murray, renowned pastor and author of the early 19th century, penned a very profound statement on waiting and depending on God. He wrote, "…because Christians do not know their relation to

God of absolute poverty and helplessness, that they have no sense of the need of absolute and unceasing dependence, or the unspeakable blessedness of continual waiting on God. But when once a believer begins to see it, and consent to it, that he by the Holy Spirit must each moment receive what God each moment works, waiting on God becomes his brightest hope and joy." (Murray, 2014) Murray is basically saying that if we truly knew and understood our relation to the Father, if we only knew how we in and of ourselves are incapable of giving ourselves what we really need, we would know that it is His desire to provide the absolute best for us here on earth, but more so for eternity. God has His eyes on us for the sole purpose of loving and saving us. Everything else is either secondary or immaterial. While He is preparing you and me for eternity, it would do us well to learn how to wait on Him to work His good works in us and for us. As far as your season of blooming is concerned, it is basically a given. You will not always stay where you are unless you choose to. God wants people that He can abundantly bless. Will that person be you? His name will be glorified, and people will testify of the goodness of the Lord. Someone once said that man's extremities are God's opportunities. Nothing is too hard for God. Wait on the Lord. Never shall He fail! While you wait on the Lord, the great Master Gardner, Himself, has been making sure that everything you need to survive above your circumstances is intact. All the necessary sustenance that you need to thrive in conditions different from your winter season, He has already set in place. In the fullness of His perfect timing, you will experience a new season of growth and bloom. God will bring you into this season to prosper you, to expand you, to position you, to prepare you to do great things in His name. The winter season is rough, but you will come through it. God sees something in you that you are unable to see unless He brings you through a time of difficult or extreme conditions. Difficulty has a unique way of bringing out the best and worst in us. In this case, God wants to bring out your best.

In other words, He would not have even bothered with you had He not known your spiritual potential. God sees so much value in you that He has already designed a specific purpose for you. His plan is to get you to live out your purpose according to His plan. When your plans have failed and continue to keep you from moving forward, God's plan has been there all along. The defining element in allowing God room to work His plan in you is to "surrender." It is such a difficult position to assume when you would rather be in charge. But, God wants to be the head of your life. He wants to have dominion over you and me. He wants to be Lord over our hearts.

As long as you and I want to do everything our way and on our timing, the more we get in the way of God exacting His will in our lives. The most important thing that any of us can do is to turn our lives over to Jesus. What I really mean is that we need to give up control. By the way, if being in control is really working, then why is it necessary to come to God for help? It seems to me that it is probably not working. I believe that the Creator, who from the beginning, made everything new in the earth, can also create a new thing in our lives. What do you say to that?

While you are thinking about the spring season of your life, I am pretty sure you would like to know for certain what to expect. I wish that I could tell you that everything you prayed for will be given to you, but I can't. What I can tell you is that there are some promises you stand on. One such promise is found in Hebrews 10:23

(MSG) "So let's do it—full of belief, confident that we're presentable inside and out. Let's keep a firm grip on the promises that keep us going. He always keeps his word." God has given us promises to not just memorize and rehearse, but rather to plant them into our hearts to the point of absolute belief. Part of the problem with many Christians today is that they do not literally take God at His word. I was one of those people.

We have been so deceived by the enemy that we do not believe the efficacy and veracity of God's Word as we should. Like Himself, God's Word is immutable. It cannot change. If He promised, He is faithful to perform it. The problem lies with us. We have put too many stipulations on His promises coming to pass. The bottom line is that God's Word is truth. Your faith is the key to believing Him. I hope that I am making myself clear. What have you earnestly and fervently prayed? The last time I checked,

God still answers prayers. Every prayer that comes from the heart, God will answer. One way that I have learned to pray is asking God to show me in His word what He wants me to know, then help my prayers line up with what He is showing me in His word. I often tell God that I don't want to waste my breath or time praying for anything that is not according to His will or His word.

As you are waiting to awesomely blossom, I would like to encourage you to ask God what areas in your life would He like to make over? Ask Him to help you better understand His will for your life by showing you in His word. Another promise in the Bible that has been helpful to me is found in Psalm 62:5 KJV, "My soul, wait thou only upon God; for my expectation is from him." When the Holy Spirit led me to that verse, I contemplated it for a very long time. What it said to me was to not look to anyone for my answer. Do I depend or place my confidence in anything or anyone for the answers that He alone can give? It made me realize that as long as I wait on the Lord, I can expect Him to answer because He became my highest expectation.

In many cases, I have not always wanted to wait. Waiting is an inconvenience when you have a demand for something that you need. Waiting seems to make us restless. However, the more we understand that God has our best interest at heart, the more confidence we should have while waiting on Him. In my opinion, what seems to be the problem with the waiting process is the threat of things falling apart if God does not answer instantly. How many times has something really fallen apart because God did not answer? When I look over my life, I can see many instances when God said "no." It wasn't my choice answer, but He did answer.

If we sought God as much as we seek after His gifts, we would probably hear from Him more often. We want God's resources, but how deeply and passionately do we want His heart? You and I do not like to be used, so why do we think it is ok to use God? Maybe you and I may not have intentionally used God, but we humans have a habit of consistently asking for material things instead of those things of greater value, such as love, patience, kindness, goodness, long-suffering, etc. (see Galations 5:22). On the other hand, when we desire the characteristics of God and ask Him to develop them in our character, He will most assuredly do so in copious measure. This kind of request is of great value.

You can tell what a man values not based on what he owns, but what is owning him. That simply means that if a person is possessed with having this and that all the time, then those things probably rule his or her life. If a person values what he or she has, but places more value on the Person who gave those things, then more than likely, the individual desires the Giver over the gifts. Now don't get me wrong, gifts are beautiful. That's why God gave them to us to use. Whether they are spiritual gifts or earthly gifts, God gave them to us so that we can share them with others. Therefore, ownership is not really ownership when it comes down to it. Ownership becomes "loanership" because gifts are given so that they can be shared. So, before you begin your season of blossoming, God has to make sure you are planted and rooted in Him, not just what you can get from Him. When He has fully examined you, He will be able to distinguish between the soul who is truly satisfied with Him, rather than the soul who finds greater satisfaction with materialistic things from Him. Ask yourself, "What or who do I desire in my heart more than anything?"

And anything that we desire in our heart, the Lord is willing to give. Anything you ask? Yes, anything! How do I know? Well, the Bible is crystal clear. It reads, "Therefore I say unto you, what things soever ye desire, when ye pray, believe that ye receive them, and ye shall have them." Mark 11:24 KJV. Can I dare to say that you want the things of God! When you believe that God is going to deliver on His promises, then there is nothing for you to fear. In fact, I feel pretty confident that if I ask for the things of God according to His word and by faith, I will have them. You can also take God at His word. The cool thing about taking God at His word is that it helps you to not be in a hurry! When you believe that God's timing is perfect, you are willing to wait on Him. Are you willing to wait on God to bring you full circle into your season of being an awesome blossom?

Since we have made it back to talking about blossoming, let's examine the blossoming process of a tulip. Before the tulip begins to blossom, it has already received what it needs from the bulb. However, there are culprits that may come along to agitate, corrode, or even destroy the growing tulip. The culprits are mold, slugs, snails, or even bulb rot. These culprits attach themselves to the root structure of the tulip and cause the tulip to be in grave danger of blossoming to its full potential.

Lauren Miller, writer and gardener explained, "The most serious diseases that affect tulips include those caused by fungi, simple plants that cannot produce their own food. Fungi lack chlorophyll, become parasites to plants…" (Miller, 2014) Slugs also feed on tubers and bulbs. These very same culprits exist in real life and show up in real situations. They don't produce anything on their own, so they look for growing and blossoming people to whom they can attach to drain and destroy. Be wary of these people. On your way to your spring season, before you get there, and while you are being prepared to blossom, you may encounter some culprits to agitate, corrode, or even destroy you or what God has place in your mind about what is possible for you. They are naysayers, critical and negative people who are like parasites. They are takers and not givers. They will take your enthusiasm. They will take your dream and undermine it. They will take your joy. They will take your confidence. Then there are some people like slugs and snails who move slowly but who deliberately eat away at you. Some other culprits are disbelief, self-doubt, procrastination, or dwelling on past failures. Quiet as it's kept, these culprits are the worst of all kinds especially if the parasites are from within. Negative self-talk will corrode and eat you alive down to the core. Not only that, it will have you believing the worst possible thing about yourself. Sometimes these people or dispositions sneak upon you without you realizing that you have been sought after. There's a biblical promise that God gives us when we are caught off guard by the enemy and his agents. It is found in Isaiah 59:19. It reads, "When the enemy shall come in like a flood, the Spirit of the Lord will lift up a standard against him." The enemy cannot stand a chance when the Spirit gets ahold of him. Just like the mold, slugs, or snails can't stand a chance when the gardener uses killing agents to destroy the enemies of the tulip. The Lord will not allow the enemy to prevail against you. If you have found yourself surrounded by or indulging in thinking such as I have mentioned, there are several things you can do to eradicate them.

1. The first thing is to acknowledge the source of negativity which may include people, places, things,

or thoughts. In other words, be aware of triggers, cues, and keywords that alert you that the source of negativity is present so that you can counter them with the most appropriate and effective response. I call this your **PCR**: **P**ositive **C**ounter **R**esponse. In the table below, write down common triggers in the first column. In the second column, write down a positive counter response. Here's an example:

Source of Negativity/Trigger	Positive Counter Response
Thought: This day has already started out wrong.	I may not be able to control what happens today, but I can certainly control how I respond.
Person: Feeling ridiculed by a peer, colleague, or family member.	What a person thinks of me is none of my business. What I think of myself is what matters the most.
Place: I detest coming home. It is not a welcoming place.	I give myself permission to address what bothers me and to seek healthy solutions with my family members.

Your negativity triggers may differ from the example above. Write your responses in the space below:

You must also tell yourself to not take anything anyone does personally. When you take something someone is doing personally, you are basically giving them permission to control your reaction. What a person does or says has nothing to do with you. People have the right to be who they are. Just like you have the right to be who you are. If what someone is saying or doing does not sit well with you, you have the right to ask them to stop. But, whatever you do, do not make yourself the target of their attack. Even if it seems that they are attacking you, you can say to yourself, "I don't believe what that person is saying, and I will not receive anything they speak as truth." You can neutralize anyone's negativity by healthy self-talk. I do it a lot of times. Even when someone unintentionally says something that counters what I believe about myself, or what God says is possible for me, I quickly say to myself, "I don't receive that. I believe what God says."

2. Secondly, you must remove yourself from anyone who breathes negativity over you. People who breathe negativity breed negativity. If you cannot physically remove yourself from that person's presence, then you can pray silently and ask God to

shelter you from the harm of that person or individual. Additionally, you must learn and practice how to find space in your mind to retreat. It took me a long time to learn how to do it, but I've gotten so much better at it. I want you to become an expert at securing a safe place for yourself.

3. Take advantage of resources around you that will fertilize your creativity, dream, aspiration, desire, or goal. One of the greatest resources available to most of the world is that of the Internet. You can read and listen to all kinds of books, podcasts, and articles. YouTube is loaded with videos that can inspire and motivate you. Sometimes, you can find websites that create communities for people who have shared interests. You have to become proactive in your process. Fill your mind, time, and heart with material and information that will feed you down to

your roots. Check your local library for free workshops, seminars, or development training. Your assignment for this segment is to create growth opportunity with what you already have. You have to believe before you manifest. Where you put your focus is where you will arrive. If you focus on the fungus of negativity, then you may very well populate more fungal negativity. Try focusing on the cure rather than the culprit.

In the space below, I would like for you to come up with seven words that you will use for your own "Word for the day". For one week, your focus will be on that one word which will help guide you in what you say, do, and think. For example: My word for the day is: unstoppable. All day my thoughts, words, and actions will help me to be unstoppable. Write your seven words in the spaces below:

1._____

2._____

3._____

4._____

5. _____

6._____

7._____

Your focus word will be helpful while waiting to blossom. Waiting is a necessary step in the process of developing anything sustainable. If you will partner with God while you are waiting, your waiting will not be in vain. Your relationship with God will become more intimate. Your faith will increase. Your mind will be clearer. Your attitude will be improved. You will become more productive. You are in a good place. It may not feel like it right now, but you are. I have been there. Everything that has transpired until now has been absolutely necessary

for your season of blossom.

"If an apple blossom or a ripe apple could tell its own story, it would be, still more than its own, the story of the sunshine that smiled upon it, of the winds that whispered to it, of the birds that sang around it, of the storms that visited it, and of the motherly tree that held it and fed it until its petals were unfolded and its form developed." -
Lucy Larcom

Chapter 7
Awesome Blossom

If you could look into your future, what would you see? In the previous chapter, we discussed waiting on God to bring you into your season of blossom. What does that look like to you? Your season of blossom? On the lines on the next page, I would like for you to write in your own words (descriptively) what picture you see as you contemplate fulfilling your goals and dreams?

Write: When I think about my dreams, vision, or goals being fulfilled, I see...

Now that you have given yourself a snapshot of what that blossomed person looks to you, the next thing that I want you to do is to examine one point you made in the description above, and turn that point into a goal. Once you have established what that goal is, the next thing that I would like for you to do is decide that you will do at least one thing towards that goal every day for the next thirty (30) days. Before you jump right into it, let me share with you what I did. I have been working on my second business for the past four years, I have seen marginal growth. This led to some discouragement and subsequently low drive to keep pushing. However, I kept trying to the best of my ability. One evening, I received a text message from a very good friend to listen to an audio recording on YouTube. A couple of days later, I did, and my mind was blown at the encouragement and focus that the speaker put on completing tasks for success. After listening to the audio, I prayed and asked God what area of my life or what task did He think that I should focus on for the next thirty days? Two days later, it resonated in my spirit to finish writing the very book you are reading right now. At this point in the chapter, I am still within that thirty day commitment to write every day for thirty days. As I am writing now, I am on day twenty. I have ten more days to complete this assignment. The determining factor that has kept me to the task is that I covenanted with God. Additionally, I asked Him to do something super amazing, super crazy out of the box if I kept my end of the covenant. So far, so good! Now, let me be clear. God is a covenant-keeping God, He is the one who keeps the covenant. We are the ones who agree to the covenant. I am convinced that writing this book is so much bigger and powerful than just making an accomplishment, or telling my story. This book-writing assignment started in 2012, and God never allowed me to rest comfortably knowing that I had not completed what He had given me to do. So, the more I think about it, the more I realize that writing this book is about the power and authority of God in my life, and how important it is to trust Him as I walk in obedience. I know for sure that God takes nothing and makes something out of it that will bring Him glory. This book is being written by inspiration of God. This is His project. I am just the vessel He is using to tell what He is doing in my life and in the lives of those reading this book. The reason I shared this story with you is because I am sure that God has planted in you a dream, a goal, a desire, a vision, or whatever He has appointed you to do. If you have been hemming and hawing about this that or the other thing, and have not completed what God has given you to do, now is your chance to square it up with God. Seek His face in prayer and listen for the answer. He will tell you exactly what you are supposed to do and when to start. The thirty day initiative is going to jumpstart you off on a new plan and purpose. You have nothing to lose, but everything to gain to get you in gear for better productivity which opens the ways for you to blossom.

As a productivity coach, I am often helping individuals with life coaching. I learned of a technique that I share with my clients. I am not sure who to give the credit to, but it has a lot of merit to it. It is called, "shine the sink". Let me explain: "Shine the sink" is a code phrase for getting at least one area of your home, life, office, garage, etc. in order. Not only do you get it in order, you keep it in order. The premise behind shine the sink is clearing out clutter. Do you have any area of your life, house, office, garage, storage area that is cluttered? If you do, then "shine the sink" is for you. Clutter has the tendency to affect the body in many different ways, mainly stress. The clutter itself causes more stress then being stressed about what is keeping you from clearing it out. Clutter populates more clutter. When you have a cluttered environment or mind, you flat out cannot think straight. Your thoughts are fragmented, which makes it difficult to follow through on other assignments that are more important. So first thing is first. De-clutter a *small* area that has gotten out of control. Please do not take on a big job. It can be something as small as a dresser, dish washer, cabinet, etc. The reason why I am asking you to take a small area is because I want you to successfully accomplish this task. If you take on something too big, you may get stressed out about it or maybe even frustrated. Once you have decided what area you would like to "shine the sink" (de-clutter), the next thing to do is pick a day and time that works for you. After you pick a day and time, I would like for you to estimate how much time you think it would take for you to accomplish the task. Make sure you

are being reasonable. Once you have you day, time, and

how long it will take for you to complete the task, I would

like for you get started. But before you do, please keep in

mind that you are to be relaxed. This is not supposed to be

a stressful task. Turn on some music or something

inspirational. If it helps to light a scented candle, you are

welcome to do that as well. After your time is up, and you

have completed the task, I want you to stand back to

admire how the area looks. After doing so, I would like for

you record in the space below, how it made you feel; what

thoughts went through your mind; why did you choose that

particular area. Write here:

_____

_____

_____

_____

_____

_____

_____

_____

This next step is going to cost you a little something. Now that you have the selected area completed, you now have to keep it clean. The moment you put something in that area that doesn't belong there, or it is out of its proper place, I want you to remind yourself to, "shine the sink."

The primary reason why I am including "shine the sink" in this chapter is because I want to help you develop a habit of clearing your mind as you would a physical environment. As I've stated earlier, when your mind is clear, you can better discern the voice of God. When there is clutter all around you, it really affects your ability to hear, process, or respond efficiently and in a timely manner. Consequently, junk can impede your overall productivity. You are more prone to procrastinate. Your energy level is affected. You tend to loathe the simplest tasks. Besides, organizing an area that is in disarray will bring a special kind of peace and calm you hadn't experienced in a long time. I promise you, things change. Many of my clients can attest to this. Clearing your mind will also help you to be able to recognize when God is speaking to you. If you are having trouble hearing God's voice, there may be a couple of things you may need to clear out. If there is willful disobedience, that will hinder you from hearing God's voice. If you are placing higher priority on what you want rather than what God wants for you, you may have trouble hearing His voice. If you are compromising on moral principles, you may not hear when God is speaking to you. The point I am making is that you have to clear up clutter in your life. Only you and God know what those areas are. When you put yourself in better position to hear, His voice becomes clearer above any other voice. His voice is distinct and will never conflict with what He is showing you in His word. It is God's desire for us all to be in good health, mentally, physically, emotionally, and spiritually. Paul wrote in III John 1:2 (KJV) "Beloved, I wish above all things that thou mayest prosper and be in health, even as thy soul prospereth." You see, God wants only the best for you. So you would want to make sure that you are at peace in these areas. When we are intentional in making sure those areas are in alignment with the will of God, we make room for Him to speak and commune with us in depth. God can commune with us in many different ways using different methods. He may send someone your way, or He may open up an opportunity for you to learn and grown in an area where you have demonstrated a need for development. I really saw this truth come to pass leading up to completing this book. God has a way of taking separate and seemingly unrelated events and then connecting them full-circle to bring about His will and plans. For example, as I mentioned in an earlier chapter, a friend of mine invited me to come along with her on a gratitude art journaling journey. After we were done with that, a few days later it seemed, I received a text message to take a look at a YouTube video that really gave me a burst of energy, and caused me to enter into a covenant agreement with God about this book. Subsequent to that, the night before Thanksgiving, I met and talked with a lady about goals and aspirations for nearly two hours in her van. The following week, my business property owner came by and shared some very powerful words with me about goals and dreams. That very same day, I went to a meeting and got confirmation on launching my new product line, Kura Hydrating Hair System. The crazy thing about all these events were that they are isolated and unrelated to each other. But what I didn't get right away was that maybe just maybe God was testing me to see whether I would be opened to each of these God-inspired interactions. As I have said to a couple of friends, I believe that the launching of my product line was just God's way of letting me know that I have to step my foot in the water. In other words, I had to take action with the current information or opportunity that He gave me. If God can trust you with small opportunities, then He will be able to trust you with opportunities of epic proportion. So, hurry now, get busy and "shine the sink"! Put things in order so that you'll recognize when God is putting things in order for you. When God puts things in order for His children, He could do it all at one time, but in many cases, He doesn't. I really don't know why exactly, but I can make a pretty good educated guess. I believe that if God did everything so suddenly for us all of the time, and all at one time, we would never learn how to respect and honor Him for who He is. We would confuse who He is with what He can do. We would never fully grow in faith, patience, grace, and waiting. God is totally about relationship. He wants to relate to us and relate with us. He also wants us to want the same. When God takes His time in bringing everything together for your season of blossoming, it's because He is working out everything for your good (Romans 8:28). Sometimes, this is a hard pill to swallow. I have since learned what it means to know that God is working out everything for my good. Recently, I was led to 1Thessalonians 5:16-18 again. "Rejoice always, pray continuously, give thanks in every circumstance, for this is the will of God for you in Christ Jesus." I read further and discovered that the "rejoice always" is more than an expression of emotion. The NIV Commentary helped me to understand that it is an expression of experiencing God as active and at work in my life. The fact that God is working in my life is just cause to rejoice always. What I want you to think about is that God is at work in your life too. He is working everything out in your life for your good! That is WORTH rejoicing. If God is always working, then we ought to always be rejoicing.

The more I think about the idea of rejoicing, it makes me think about the joy of the Lord. Jesus admonishes His readers in John 15 to remain in Him. He said when we remain in Him, his joy will remain in us, and our joy would be full. When was the last time you felt full of the joy of the Lord? If you are not full, then something happened. Something changed. You must have apparently moved away from the true Vine. How do I know? Because God doesn't change. He declared, "I am God and I change not." Malachi 3:6. So, He didn't move. You have either moved by virtue of your own thoughts, or by implementing your own action plan, or by second guessing the veracity and application of God's word in your life. When you move away from God, it becomes increasingly difficult to recognize His voice, or to feel His Presence. As the branch, we are to remain in Him, the Vine. A person who remains in Christ, and knows that God is doing mighty works in his or her life gets to have overflowing joy. In spite of the current circumstance, the joy of the Lord keeps overflowing in that individual's life. That's what blossoming is all about. It is all about the joy of the Lord. "Do not grieve, for the joy of the Lord is your strength." Nehemiah 8:10. Your awesome blossom season is upon you. This is where you do as Joel Osteen suggests. He argues that if we are to see the manifestation of God's power wow us, then we are going to have to take the limits off God: Dare to stretch our faith. We'll have to dare to believe. We must dare to take God out of the box. Dare to pray God-sized prayers. Once we have released God from our pre-conceived notions, He can really do what He does best. I am willing to bet that you have held God hostage in a box for a long time now. It's time to let Him out of your imagination box. Let Him have full control over your life in reality. God only wants the best for you. He is with you. You cannot get away from God. "Be strong, be courageous. Be not dismayed, for the Lord your God is with you wherever you go. (Joshua 1:9). God will cause everywhere you go to be a place and opportunity to blossom you. God wants to show you off. He wants you to show the world His matchless love. He wants you to be a reflection and showcase of His glory. Your blossoming season is upon you. God is still in the blessing business. Just like He promised ancient Israel that He will allow them to possess the land which He had given them. God wants you to take possession of that which He has given you. This is the time of refreshing, restoration, and redemption. It doesn't matter how long it has been since you have had a season of renewal. Even if you have been cut all the way down, that is no big deal to God. Just as the word says that God will cause a sprout to come forth from the stump of a tree, He will cause you to spring forth from the stump of setbacks, from the stump of disappointments, from the stump of rejection, from the stump of illness, from the stump of financial ruin, from the stump of spiritual apathy. Not only will God cause you to spring forth with newness, but He will cause you to spring forth, and your shoots will never die. That is to say your future generations will also spring up. Job 14:1 (HCSB) states, "There is hope for a tree: If it is cut down, it will sprout again, and its shoots will not die." Imagine how that would be? This is what God wants to do for you. What you have to realize is that your blossoming season has nothing do with you reaching a certain goal, or obtaining some material thing, but it has everything to do with *who* you become in Christ Jesus. As the bible explains in 2 Corinthians 5:17 (CSV), "Therefore, if anyone is united with the Messiah, he is a new creation — the old has passed; look, what has come is fresh and new!" God's creative work still continues as God seeks to accomplish new things in us. You may feel that your relationship with Christ is intact, and it very well may be. But last time I checked, we all have some "other" issues that God has to purge from us. I know this for a fact. I am currently experiencing my blossoming season even as I am completing this book. Writing this book is an act of obedience on my part. I believe that for every individual reading this book, God will bring them to a place healing and restoration; blossoming and blooming. I am seeing

God accomplish in me things that absolutely looked impossible, and for the most part, I had laid aside. I admonish you to not take anything for granted. Give thanks in every circumstance. Your blossoming season is upon you. God will bring you back to a place of full restoration and bloom. "Then all your people will be righteous; they will possess the land forever; they are the branch I planted, the work of My hands, so that I may be glorified." Isaiah 60:21

You have arrived at the end of this book. During this reading experience, we've journeyed together through our difficulties and have learned much. Because you are the work of God's hands, your best is yet to come! If you are still in your fall season, don't let that bother you because your present circumstance, even through the most extreme conditions of life's transitions, is just a temporary period that God is using to guide you from a dormant fall season of bareness to a spring season of beautiful incredible blossoms. Your fall season was never meant to define where you are. God used it as a vehicle to move you from a place of dormancy to a place of awesome blossom. Your fall season was never meant to take you out, but it was meant to take you up to a place of absolute surrender, trust, and absolutely abiding in God. Your fall season was never meant to overcome you, but it was meant to make you an overcomer. No longer succumbing to defeat, despair, or disappointment, but to lead you on a victory parade riding on the train of Christ's triumph. Christ's triumph is your triumph! Your fall season was never meant to make you want to give up, but was meant to make you press forward. Your fall season was never meant to pound you, but to prosper you. Your fall season was never meant to desecrate you but to elevate you. Your fall season was necessary for your blossoming season. Your blossom season is upon you! Rise up! Your blossom season is upon

you! Shine bright! Your blossom season is upon you!

Spring forth! Your blossom season is upon you! Praise

God! May God be ever so gracious to you *When Tulips*

Bloom! Peaceful Blessings~

"After your season of suffering, God in all His grace will RESTORE, CONFIRM, STRENGTHEN and ESTABLISH you" 1 Peter 5:10

Bible texts are taken from the King James Version of the Holy Bible unless otherwise cited. Quotes appearing at the beginning of each chapter are taken from www.goodreads.com .

References

Hahn, J. (2002). *Light for My Path for Women.* Uhrichsville: Humble Creek.

Ionatti, M. (2014, November 25). *When Should I Plant My Spring Blooming Bulbs?* Retrieved from About.com: http://gardening.about.com/od/floweringbulbs/a/Planting_Bulbs.htm

Miller, L. (2014, November 10). *Home Guides.* Retrieved from San Francisco Gate: http://homeguides.sfgate.com/tulip-fungus-25425.html

Murray, A. (2014, November 21). *Waiting on God.* Retrieved from World Invisible: http://www.worldinvisible.com/library/murray/waiting/waiting.htm

Swope, R. (2013). *A Confident Heart.* Grand Rapids: Revell .

Tozer, A. (n.d.). Following Hard After God. In A. Tozer, *The Pursuit of God* (pp. 12-13). Risburg: Christian Publications, Inc.

Warren, R. (2014, May 21). *The Importance of Understanding God's Love.* Retrieved from Daily Hope with Rick Warren: http://rickwarren.org/devotional/english/the-importance-of-understanding-god-s-love

Warren, R. (n.d.). *Daily Hope with Rick W.*

What's In a Name? (2014, November 25). Retrieved from Journey
North:
http://www.learner.org/jnorth/tm/tulips/WhatsInAName.html

Special thanks and recognition given to Barbara Upshaw at
Aura Graphics and Design for capturing my concept in
creating the book cover design, Cheryl Bowne for record-
time editing assistance, Samiah Alexander for giving me a
polished look for the About the Author photograph, and to
my son-in-love, Ryan M. Felton for being my right hand
main man who always gets things done with a willing
spirit. Much love!

Made in the USA
Charleston, SC
12 April 2015